Explode The Code® 2nd Edition

Essential lessons for phonics mastery

8

Nancy Hall • Rena Price

EDUCATORS PUBLISHING SERVICE
Cambridge and Toronto

Cover art: Hugh Price
Text illustrations: Jamie Maxfield, Paula Becker

Printed in Mayfield, PA, in August 2022
ISBN 978-0-8388-7808-8

10 11 12 13 PAH 25 24 23 22

CONTENTS

Lesson 1

A **suffix** is an ending added to a root to change the meaning slightly.
-ness and *-less* are suffixes

Circle the endings and write the syllables in the squares.

1. kind(ness)	k i n d	n e s s	2
2. thankfulness	_ _ _ _ _	_ _ _	_ _ _ _	
3. bottomless	_ _ _	_ _ _ _	_ _ _ _	
4. wilderness	_ _ _	_ _ _ _	_ _ _ _	
5. regardless	_ _	_ _ _ _	_ _ _ _	
6. foolishness	_ _ _ _	_ _ _	_ _ _ _	
7. helpfulness	_ _ _ _	_ _ _	_ _ _ _	

Now count the syllables in each word and write the number in the margin.
(Tap the desk to help yourself hear the syllables.)

Unscramble the syllables to make a word that fits the meaning.

a feeling of being alone too much = ness / li / lone → <u>loneliness</u>

Remember: *i* before many endings says /ē/ or is short, even though it ends the syllable.

1. having no bottom = tom / bot / less → _____

2. an act of assisting or being helpful = ful / help / ness → _____

3. something foolish = ness / sil / li → _____

4. having no power = less / pow / er → _____

5. refusing to change one's mind = born / stub / ness → _____

6. a large, wild area where no people live = wil / ness / der → _____

7. not worth much = ue / val / less → _____

Circle the roots and complete the sentence with the word.

	(stubborn) (stubbornness)	Tracy is a very _stubborn_ girl. Her _stubbornness_ often gets her into trouble. **Note:** When the root ends in *e*, it usually drops the *e* if the suffix begins with a vowel (*strange* + *er* = *stranger*.) When the root ends in *y*, the *y* changes to *i* when you add a suffix (*gloomy* + *ness* = *gloom<u>iness</u>*.)
1.	stranger strangeness	There was a _____ about the old house that made even a _____ shiver.
2.	polite politeness	_____ is something that teachers like. If you are _____, they will often praise you.
3.	noise noiseless	A buzzing fly makes a lot of _____. I wish someone would develop a _____ fly.
4.	value valueless	Many people put great _____ on their cars. I have an old rusted car that is _____, but I love it anyway.
5.	slippery slipperiness	The _____ of the icy sidewalks made it too _____ to walk without boots.
6.	gloomy gloominess	The _____ of the day began to affect us all. Why can't the sun shine on such a _____ day?
7.	reckless recklessness	Eric was a very _____ bike rider. His _____ caused him to smash into his mother's parked car.

Find the word that means the opposite of the given word and write it in the boxes.

A word that means the opposite is called an **antonym.**

weightless   kindness   smoothness
rudeness   careless   helpfulness
hopeless   fearless   emptiness

1. Roughness: `s m o o t h n e s s`

2. Cruelty:

3. Careful:

4. Politeness:

5. Heavy:

6. Fullness:

7. Afraid:

Circle the correct word below.

Look at the suffix *-less* and think about the words we have used with this suffix. A sleeveless dress is one _____ sleeves. You now know that the suffix *-less* means "_____."

-ness means "a state of being"; for example, *happi<u>ness</u>* means "being happy."

1. When you have been home alone for a long time, will you feel a sense of

   (loneliness)   or   largeness?

2. When you cannot change something that has happened and you wish you could, might you feel

   powerless   or   politeness?

3. It is a splendid day with sun and blue sky. Would you describe the day as

   countless   or   cloudless?

4. When you taste a piece of lemon and it makes you wrinkle your nose, is it

   the sourness   or   the snugness?

5. On a windy, stormy night a huge tree blew down near your house but nothing was hurt. Do you have a feeling of

   thanklessness   or   thankfulness?

6. It has rained all week and even the towels and the sheets on your bed feel wet. Is what you feel in the air

   deafness   or   dampness?

7. The dog and cat get into a fight and tip over Mom's best vase, smashing it to bits. Mom is angry when she gets home. Are you

   blameless   or   softness?

6

Put an X after the headline that matches each picture.

1. Mouse Powerless with Cat ☐

   Dog's Politeness Wins Cat ☐

2. Brainless Idea Helps Humankind ☐

   Brightness Of Moon Unusual Tonight ☐

3. Glassy Ice Cream Wins for Smoothness ☐

   Grassy Hill Chosen for Festival ☐

4. Stubbornness of Mule—Can't Be Budged ☐

   Steepness of Road Makes for a Hard Race ☐

5. Reckless Driver Stopped for Speeding ☐

   Reckless Tail Sweeps Table Top ☐

6. Pete Powerless to Stop Earthquake ☐

   Helpfulness of Pet Aids Child ☐

7. Kindness to Others Is Rewarded ☐

   Carelessness Results in Lost Bracelet ☐

Yes or no?

	Yes	No
1. Is it foolishness to help a friend?	☐	☐
2. If your full cup is bottomless, will you ever be thirsty?	☐	☐
3. Can you get holes in the elbows of a sleeveless sweater?	☐	☐
4. Is the wilderness slowly being destroyed by humans?	☐	☐
5. When you help your friend do her homework, is it kindness?	☐	☐
6. If you never thanked your sister, would she praise your politeness?	☐	☐
7. Is it careless to leave your new bike in the middle of the driveway?	☐	☐

Rena's Cool Idea

It was a hot, cloudless day in July. Dampness hung in the air. The flies buzzed slowly.

It was very humid and too hot to move. Even swimming in the pool was foolishness because the water was so warm.

Everyone felt listless—but not Rena! She picked up the phone and said, " I want to order one truckload, please."

Her friend Tess laughed, but soon, Rena's silliness turned to cleverness. A truck arrived and dumped five hundred pounds of ice in the pool!

"Thanks for your kindness, Cousin Gene," said Rena.

"Maybe I'll take a swim, too," said her cousin. "After all, what good is having an ice company if you can't enjoy the coolness?"

1. Circle all the words that end with the suffix *-ness* or *-less.*

2. Underline the words that tell why this day was so bad.

3. When you have a problem like Rena's and you don't know how to solve it, you feel h __ __ __ less.

4. Would you praise Rena for her rudeness or her smartness? (Circle one.)

5. If you had been Rena, what would you have done? (Circle one.)

   a. Blamed the weather forecaster for not warning you?

   b. Rung the fire alarm to let your friends know about the burning heat?

   c. Rubbed your skin with frozen ice cream cones?

   d. Other _____

   _____

Lesson 2

Some suffixes do not sound like their spelling.

    -ous says /us/ as in *fam<u>ous</u>*.   *-or* says /er/ as in *sail<u>or</u>*.

Circle the suffixes. Then write the syllables in the squares.
Note: sometimes the way you divide a word into syllables is different from the way you divide it into a root and a suffix.

1. act(or)		<u>a</u> c	<u>t o</u> r	2
2. inventor	_ _	_ _ _	_ _ _	
3. marvelous	_ _ _	_ _ _	_ _ _	
4. spectator	_ _ _ _	_ _	_ _ _	
5. advisor	_ _	_ _	_ _ _	
6. glamorous	_ _ _ _	_ _	_ _ _	
7. nervous		_ _ _	_ _ _ _	

Now count the syllables in each word and write the number in the margin.
Remember to tap!

10

Unscramble the syllables to make a word that fits the meaning.

one who collects things = col / tor / lec > collector

1. very large or great = dous / men / tre > _____

2. one who inspects things = spec / in / tor > _____

3. very funny = mor / hu / ous > _____

4. willing to give; unselfish = gen / ous / er > _____

5. a college teacher = pro / sor / fes > _____

6. someone who comes to see someone = tor / vis / i > _____

7. full of poison = ous / son / poi > _____

Circle the roots and complete the sentence with the word.

⊙poison⊙ ⊙poison⊙ous	If you dump _____poisonous_____ waste into lakes and rivers, it will _____poison_____ the water you drink.	

1. | conduct
conductor | The _____ raised her baton and started to _____ the band.

2. | mountain
mountainous | The _____ state of Nevada does not have a single _____ in the south.

3. | hazard
hazardous | Campfires can be _____ in the dry woods. Are the campfires still a _____ if the woods are not dry?

4. | act
actor | The _____ closed his eyes and began to weep. He can _____ well.

5. | invent
inventor | Thomas Edison was a famous _____. He worked long hours to _____ the electric light.

6. | humor
humorous | Greta has a good sense of _____. She always tells stories in a most _____ way.

7. | edit
editor | An _____ is someone who will _____ , or correct, the book you have written.

12

Find the word that is described and write it in the boxes.

Remember: -ous says /us/.

governor	continuous	instructor
enormous	ridiculous	nervous
mountainous	spectator	collector

1. Someone who gets upset and worries easily is said to be:

2. The person who runs or governs the state:

3. Something that continues on and never stops is said to be:

4. A person who watches sports events:

5. Something that is very large is said to be:

6. A person who teaches you:

7. Something that is foolish and might be made fun of is said to be:

13

Circle the correct word below.

Look at the suffix *-or* and think about the words we have used with this suffix.

An actor is a _____ who acts. You now know that *-or* usually means "a _____ who does something."

1. If you correct a book before it's published, are you

    a sailor   or   an editor?

2. When you want to share what you have with someone else, are you

    curious   or   generous?

3. When you give someone advice and help them decide what to do, are you

    an elevator   or   an advisor?

4. When you look something over carefully to see if it is running properly, are you

    an inspector   or   a tractor?

5. If you are directing a play and telling the actors what to do, are you

    the director   or   the professor?

6. If you are very handsome and charming, are you

    enormous   or   glamorous?

7. If you are very angry at someone for something they did, are you

    fabulous   or   furious?

Put an X after the headline that matches each picture.

1. Mountainous Region Hit by Fire ☐

   Marvelous Story Told by Mayor ☐

2. Glamorous Visitor Gets Wet ☐

   Generous Donor Gives Rare Fossil ☐

3. Poisonous Snake Found on Subway! ☐

   Furious Player Leaves the Field ☐

4. Continuous Show by Shooting Stars ☐

   Conductor Travels by Steamship ☐

5. Inventor Discovers Constant Sunlight ☐

   Inventor Covers Son with Invisible Paint ☐

6. Author Writes New Book ☐

   Author Wades in Cool Brook ☐

7. Spectators Cheer Team ☐

   Enormous Mudslide Stops Traffic ☐

Yes or no?

	Yes	No
1. Is an actor a famous person?	☐	☐
2. Will a visitor stay at home?	☐	☐
3. If you are generous, will you give your friend a sandwich?	☐	☐
4. Will a governor be the conductor of the band?	☐	☐
5. If the land is mountainous, can it also be enormous?	☐	☐
6. Is it foolish to use poisonous spray around birds and wildlife?	☐	☐
7. If you are curious, will you get into bed and pull the covers over your head?	☐	☐

The Mushroom Collectors

Raymond was a mushroom collector. So was his mom. Together, they liked to hike and explore new trails. Sometimes the trails were quite mountainous, sometimes even hazardous! With tremendous effort, they managed to find many different kinds of mushrooms.

Sometimes the mushrooms they found were poisonous. Raymond and his mom avoided these dangerous mushrooms and picked only delicious, non-poisonous ones. They put the mushrooms into two enormous canvas bags that they carried with them on the trails.

Were Raymond and his mom ever nervous about picking poison mushrooms by mistake? They weren't, because Raymond's mom was a famous science book editor who knew all about mushrooms. She shared what she knew with her son. Raymond then shared his knowledge about mushrooms with his science professor and some of his classmates who were curious about poisonous mushrooms. Raymond even shared the delicious ones with them when they prepared, baked, and then ate a mushroom-topped pizza at his house!

1. Circle all the words that end with the suffix *-ous* or *-or.*

2. Underline the word that means *tasty*.

3. When some is huge, it is e __ __ __ __ ous.

4. For what is Raymond's mom famous? _____

_____

5. What two things did Raymond share with his professor and classmates?

_____

Lesson 3

Suffixes change the root. *-ist* and *-ity* (pronounced as in *city*) are suffixes.

Circle the suffixes and write the syllables in the squares.
Note: Write *-ity* in one square even though it's a two-syllable suffix.

1. abil(ity)	<u>a</u>	<u>b</u> i <u>l</u>	<u>i</u> <u>t</u> y	4
2. organist	_ _	_ _ _	_ _ _	
3. druggist		_ _ _ _	_ _ _ _	
4. security	_ _	_ _	_ _ _ _	
5. locality	_ _	_ _ _	_ _ _	
6. finalist	_ _	_ _ _	_ _ _	
7. festivity	_ _ _	_ _ _	_ _ _	

Now count the syllables in each word and write the number in the margin.
Remember: *-ity* counts as two syllables.

Unscramble the syllables to make a word that fits the meaning.

	being held a prisoner	=	cap ity tiv > _captivity_

1. foolishness or lack of smartness = pid / stu / ity > _____

2. one who drives a car = tor / ist / mo > _____

3. an event that causes great harm = ca / ity / lam > _____

4. one who writes novels or books that are not about true events = el / nov / ist > _____

5. one who sings or makes music alone = ist / so / lo > _____

6. liveliness; doing something = ity / ac / tiv > _____

7. a group living and working together = mu / com / nity > _____

Circle the roots and complete the sentence with the word.

(drug)store (drug)gist	A _____ druggist _____ is a person who sells medicine in a _____ drugstore _____ .	

1.	stupid stupidity	The _____ of our team's play made us all look _____ .
2.	final finalists	All the _____ had a meeting on the _____ day of the contest.
3.	personal personality	It is my _____ opinion that her marvelous _____ makes her fun to be around.
4.	touring tourist	When he was _____ the West, he tried not to look like a _____ .
5.	major majority	The _____ reason the bill did not pass was that the _____ of the people were sick of taxes.
6.	violin violinist	The _____ put her _____ back in its case.
7.	solo soloist	A _____ is a person who sings or plays a _____ in a concert.

Find the word that is described and write it in the boxes.

motorist	pianist	ability
tourist	calamity	violinist
majority	security	druggist

1. A person who plays the piano:

2. An event that causes great harm or distress:

3. The driver of a car:

4. The skill or talent to do something:

5. A person who plays the violin:

6. Safety; being secure:

7. A person who travels for pleasure:

Circle the correct word below.

Look at the suffix *-ist* and think about the words we have used with this suffix.

An organist is a _____ who plays the organ.

You know that *-ist* usually means "a _____ who does something."

1. When you are out driving your car, are you called

   a motorist   or   a realist?

2. When you do something foolish, do you blame your

   security   or   stupidity?

3. If you have just written a book that is not about real people, are you

   a novelist   or   a pianist?

4. Is the town you live in sometimes called

   a community   or   a calamity?

5. When you see a bird in a cage where it can't escape, is it said to be in

   captivity   or   ability?

6. When something is vital and you cannot live without it, is it

   a majority   or   a necessity?

7. If you are a person who fixes teeth and takes care of dental problems, are you

   a druggist   or   a dentist?

Put an X after the headline that matches each picture.

1. Dentist Gets Fingers Stuck ☐

   Druggist Sells Rare Fingernail Clippers ☐

2. Dog Has New Ability (Can Read) ☐

   Gas Is a Modern Necessity ☐

3. First Finalist Wins Piano Contest ☐

   U.S. Tourists Visiting Paris by Plane ☐

4. Fireworks Soar at July 4 Festivity ☐

   Frog Held in Captivity by Owl ☐

5. Security Guards Save Painting ☐

   Violinist Plays Last Concert ☐

6. Snowball Activity on a Sunny Day ☐

   Ability to Tightrope Walk Across Falls ☐

7. Woodworking Artist Wins First Prize ☐

   Soloist Sings for the Queen ☐

Yes or no?

		Yes	No
1.	Are you a novelist if you have written a book about a castle with dragons?	☐	☐
2.	Do you have ability if you make six goals in the hockey game?	☐	☐
3.	Do you feel a sense of security when you have your blanket?	☐	☐
4.	Are you an artist if you draw on your bank account?	☐	☐
5.	Is cleaning your room a fabulous activity?	☐	☐
6.	Does a duck keep its chicks in captivity?	☐	☐
7.	Can a motorist be a tourist?	☐	☐

Our Town's Music Contest

Every year, our town's music community holds a contest. This activity is held to find five finalists to send to the State Music Festival in July. Tourists come from all over the state to see the best each town has to offer in musical performances.

Every year the majority of the contestants have musical ability and all want to win the contest. But there can be only five finalists. How do the judges decide on the finalists?

This year all of the finalists are soloists. Each finalist not only has musical ability, but also has a winning personality. This is a necessity when entertaining tourists!

For example, one finalist is a pianist who tells jokes in between the songs she plays. Another finalist, a saxophonist, leaves the stage to visit with members of the audience while he blows his horn. A talented guitarist, who is also the dentist in town, uses a drill to create special effects on the strings of his instrument.

Congratulations, finalists! Enjoy the festivity in July!

1. Circle all the words that end in the suffix *-ity* or *-ist*.

2. Why does the town's music community hold a yearly contest?

   _____

3. Does a soloist perform alone or with others?_____

   _____

4. Name one thing that is a necessity when entertaining tourists._____

   _____

5. Which finalist would you most want to see? Why?_____

   _____

Lesson 4 • Review

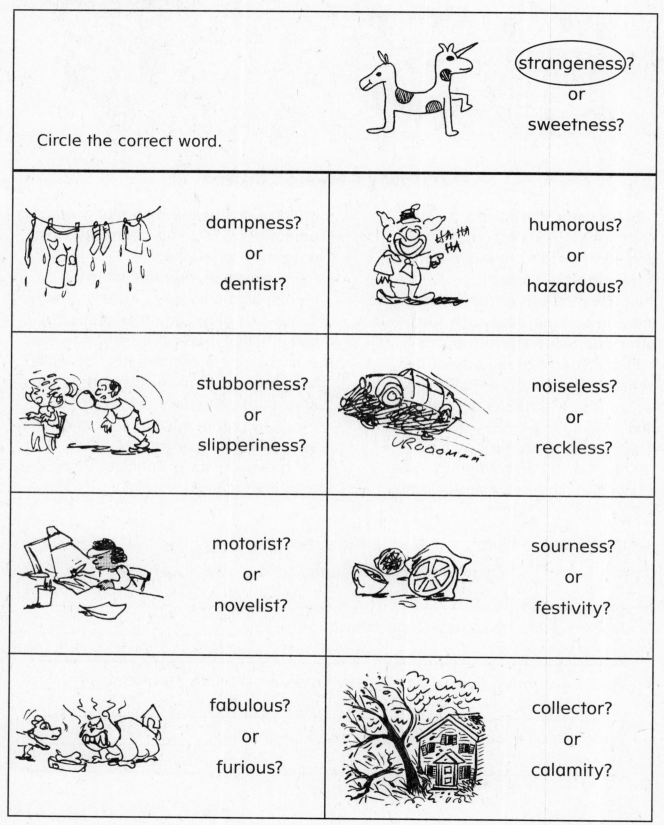

Circle the correct word.

(strangeness)?
or
sweetness?

dampness?
or
dentist?

humorous?
or
hazardous?

stubborness?
or
slipperiness?

noiseless?
or
reckless?

motorist?
or
novelist?

sourness?
or
festivity?

fabulous?
or
furious?

collector?
or
calamity?

Draw a circle around the letters that are different and fill in the blanks.

1. fear(less)
   fear(ful)

   A _____fearless_____ rat
   was trapped and ever after he was
   _____fearful_____ of traps.

2. professor
   protector

   The _____ was so afraid
   of cats that he got a large dog to be his
   _____ .

3. curious
   curiosity

   The result of the girl's _____
   about the hornet's nest made her less
   _____ about hornets after that.

4. humorous
   humorless

   Even the _____ old man
   who never laughed thought my story was
   _____ .

5. cheerfulness
   cheerless

   Grandma's _____ on such a dull,
   _____ day was a tonic to us all.

6. humanity
   humidity

   The heat and _____ seemed
   to bother all of _____ .

7. generous
   generosity

   The _____ of the rich
   conductor made us all wish we were more
   _____ .

Choose and add one of the suffixes to each underlined word.

-ous -ness -or -ist -less

When you write a *novel*, you are
called a _____novelist_____ .

1. There was great <u>danger</u> in the wild rapids. It was _____
to go rafting there.

2. His manner was very <u>gentle</u>. I admired his _____ with
the frightened cub.

3. She wore a blouse without <u>sleeves</u>. It was a _____
blouse.

4. If you <u>direct</u> the play, you are a _____.

5. It was getting <u>dark</u> outside. The _____ made it hard to
search for the lost ring.

6. You have a new <u>organ</u>. Now you will become an _____

7. Karen has a great sense of <u>humor</u>. Her jokes are so _____ .

Circle the correct meaning or definition of each underlined word.

The student's <u>ability</u> to do math in her head was amazing.

<u>Ability</u> means:
1. speed
2. being able to do something (circled)
3. need for praise

1. The little boy was <u>jealous</u> of his handsome older brother.
<u>Jealous</u> means:
1. feeling love for
2. feeling anger toward
3. feeling envy toward another

2. It was a hot, muggy day, and the <u>humidity</u> was very high.
<u>Humidity</u> means:
1. strong, cold winds
2. dampness in the air
3. kindness

3. The major's plan to attack the powerful enemy was <u>thoughtless</u>.
<u>Thoughtless</u> means:
1. well planned
2. somewhat dangerous but OK
3. without much thought or planning

4. The <u>emptiness</u> of his old home made Ricardo feel a sense of loneliness.
<u>Emptiness</u> means:
1. warm and homelike
2. a sense of being unlived in
3. a state of being excited

5. The <u>thunderous</u> applause pleased the pianist.
<u>Thunderous</u> means:
1. continuous
2. boring; tiresome
3. very loud, like thunder

6. The young <u>bicyclist</u> hoped for a cool day.
A <u>bicyclist</u> is:
1. one who repairs bikes
2. one who sells bikes
3. one who rides a bike

7. Nora's new job was the <u>opportunity</u> she had been waiting for.
<u>Opportunity</u> means:
1. a chance for advancement
2. a necessity
3. a disappointing time

Which word would you use to describe or name a person who:

~~studious~~	jealous	professor
curious	blameless	dentist
sweetness	collector	silliness

1. — studies all the time? _____studious_____

2. — likes to save baseball cards? _____

3. — fixes teeth? _____

4. — teaches college students? _____

5. — didn't do anything wrong? _____

6. — asks about things and is eager to learn more about them?

_____

7. — envies his sister because she's smarter? _____

Find and circle the words you know and then fit them into the spaces below.

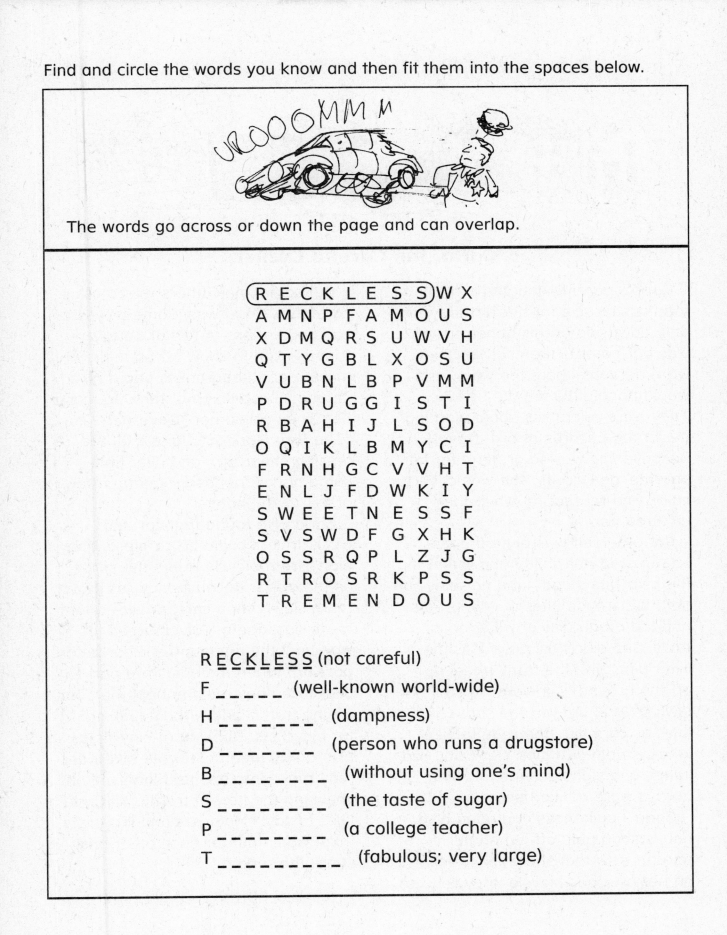

The words go across or down the page and can overlap.

```
R E C K L E S S W X
A M N P F A M O U S
X D M Q R S U W V H
Q T Y G B L X O S U
V U B N L B P V M M
P D R U G G I S T I
R B A H I J L S O D
O Q I K L B M Y C I
F R N H G C V V H T
E N L J F D W K I Y
S W E E T N E S S F
S V S W D F G X H K
O S S R Q P L Z J G
R T R O S R K P S S
T R E M E N D O U S
```

R E C K L E S S (not careful)

F _ _ _ _ _ _ (well-known world-wide)

H _ _ _ _ _ _ _ _ (dampness)

D _ _ _ _ _ _ _ (person who runs a drugstore)

B _ _ _ _ _ _ _ _ (without using one's mind)

S _ _ _ _ _ _ _ _ (the taste of sugar)

P _ _ _ _ _ _ _ _ (a college teacher)

T _ _ _ _ _ _ _ _ _ (fabulous; very large)

Carla, the Careful Cyclist

Carla's parents bought her a fabulous bicycle for her birthday. The only downside of this generous gift was her parents themselves. They were nervous about the way Carla would handle herself on the bike. They were relentless about warning her of the hazards of bike travel. Because she was so grateful for her parents' generosity, she was cheerful, calm, and reassuring when they lectured her.

Carla herself was quite fearless. She trusted her ability and found that the bike was steady and noiseless on both the smoothness of city streets and the roughness of wilderness trails. She didn't try any foolishness like riding with the front wheel up off the ground. Carla was lawful, not lawless, and obeyed the same traffic laws as cars did. She rode in bike lanes, stopped at stop signs and red lights, and signaled when turning. She always wore a bike helmet.

Carla's politeness and good bike habits soon paid off. When her parents saw that she wasn't reckless on her precious bicycle, they relaxed.

But sometimes others were not as careful as Carla was. Some bicyclists can be careless. A few of Carla's friends liked to show off on their bikes. Her stubbornness about bike safety caused some of them to tease her. They called her "Governor" or "The Bike Monitor." Carla took the teasing cheerfully, and over time some of her friends picked up a few of her lawful habits!

Carla also found that car and truck drivers could be careless. They didn't treat bicycle riders the same as motorists. Because bicycles move more slowly than cars, drivers often try to pass them. Drivers need to wait until the next lane is clear before passing. When motorists are parked at a curb, they must not open a door on the traffic side without looking for bicyclists. Honking at bicyclists is also a bad idea. A startled bike rider may move into the next lane without checking the flow of traffic. As Carla likes to say, "Motorists and bicyclists must watch out for each other and share the road."

Question Sheet

1. Circle the words that best describe Carla.

   cheerful   lawful   careless
   generous   fearless   polite

2. Write one careless thing that some of Carla's friends did.

   _____

3. Circle the letter of the main idea of the story.

   a. Carla's parents trust her.

   b. Bicyclists can be reckless.

   c. Carla is an able and careful bicyclist.

   d. Motorists and bicyclists need to share the road.

4. Do you think Carla would be a good leader? Why or why not?

   _____

   _____

   _____

5. Circle a smaller word in each word.

   noiseless   politeness   motorist   careless
   lawless   stubbornness   safety   roughness

6. Write the correct word from the story to complete each sentence.

   a. Someone who obeys the law is _____.

   b. Someone who worries is _____.

   c. Someone who takes very dangerous risks is _____.

   d. Someone who gives gifts is _____.

Lesson 5

The ending *-ture* is pronounced /chur/, as in *na<u>ture</u>*.

The ending *-ment* is pronounced /ment/, as in *mo<u>ment</u>*.

Circle the endings and write the syllables in the squares.

1. agreement	—	— — — —	— — — —	
2. improvement	— —	— — — — —	— — — —	
3. adventure	— —	— — —	— — — —	
4. argument	— —	— —	— — — —	
5. furniture	— — —	— —	— — — —	
6. departure	— —	— — —	— — — —	
7. punishment	— — —	— — —	— — — —	

Now count the syllables in each word and write the number in the margin. Remember to tap!

Unscramble the syllables to make a word that fits the meaning.

	a group of people making laws and running the city, state, or nation	=	ment gov ern

government

1.	getting better	=	prove ment im	
2.	homework	=	ment as sign	
3.	tables and chairs	=	ture ni fur	
4.	an agreement to meet at a certain time	=	ment ap point	
5.	a penalty for a crime or wrong	=	pun ment ish	
6.	an exciting event	=	ad ture ven	
7.	to make a product	=	man fac u ture	

Circle the letters that are the same and complete the sentence with the words.

(punish) (punish)ment	We _____ *punish* _____ our dog with a time-out because he needs to understand why we gave him that _____ *punishment* _____ .	

1. moist
   moisture

   The air is _____ today.
   There is _____ in the air.

2. depart
   departure

   They will _____ by the boat. The actual _____ time is 7:45 p.m.

3. astonishing
   astonishment

   We all stared in _____ as the huge balloon landed. It is _____ to see such a sight in your backyard.

4. disappointment
   appointment

   He was filled with _____ when he missed his _____ .

5. mixture
   mix

   When you _____ things together, you have a _____ .

6. prove
   improvement

   The great _____ in her health will help _____ that vitamins are helpful.

7. arrange
   arrangement

   This _____ is very good. Did you _____ it?

36

Find the word that means the same as the given word(s) and write it in the boxes.

A word that means the same as another word is called a **synonym.**

puncture	government	advancement
mixture	astonishment	imprisonment
basement	moisture	disagreement

1. Argument:

2. Improvement:

3. Captivity:

4. Surprise or amazement:

5. Dampness:

6. To punch a hole in:

7. Cellar:

Circle the correct word below.

Look at the endings *-ment* and *-ture*.

How do you pronounce *-ture*? /_____/

future   or   (furniture)?

1. When you disagree with your best friend, do you have

   an argument   or   an agreement?

2. When you draw a line with a ruler and count the inches, have you made

   a measurement   or   a manufacture?

3. When your tire blows out and is flat, is it

   a puncture   or   a picture?

4. When a criminal goes to jail, is it

   an imprisonment   or   an arrangement?

5. When you can't go skating because the ice has melted, is it

   an appointment   or   a disappointment?

6. When your home is three or four rooms in a building where other people also live, is it

   a department   or   an apartment?

7. When you break your leg, is it

   a fixture   or   a fracture?

Put an X after the headline that matches each picture.

1. Ball Players Reach Agreement ☐

   Captors Have Disagreement over Eagle ☐

2. New Department Store Opens! ☐

   Shipment Is Lost at Sea ☐

3. Actor Takes Picture in Park ☐

   Teacher Wins Government Award ☐

4. Strange Creature Captured ☐

   Shipment of Cows Stopped ☐

5. Cold Wave Hits City: Temperature Falls to Zero ☐

   President Has Temperature: Goes to Hospital ☐

6. School Assignment for Smart Dog ☐

   Homework Assignment Leads to Fame for Class ☐

7. Team Under New Management ☐

   Farmer Finds Dinosaur Bones in Pasture ☐

Yes or no?

		Yes	No
1.	Could you get a fracture skipping in a pasture?	☐	☐
2.	Can you capture your shadow?	☐	☐
3.	Is playing computer games entertainment?	☐	☐
4.	Is it a departure if someone is leaving?	☐	☐
5.	Are you glad to have a lot of assignments?	☐	☐
6.	When Dad says it's time to go to bed, are you in agreement?	☐	☐
7.	Do you live in an apartment?	☐	☐

A Sad Creature

I'll never forget the day I broke my arm. My team assignment was forward, and I had just scored a goal when I was tripped.

Instead of feeling victorious, I felt disappointment, since the fracture meant a departure from the game.

My stay in the hospital was a bit of a bad adventure. After the doctor set my fracture and put it in a cast, I had a very high temperature. The nurse punctured my good arm with a shot. The treatment must have worked because there was an improvement, and my temperature went down. I was allowed to go home.

Back at our apartment, we switched the furniture to make a better arrangement for my recovery. Stretched out on the couch, I took a picture of myself to capture my astonishment at being off the team for the rest of the season. I sent it to my teammates and our coach. What a sad creature I was!

1. Circle all the words that end with *ment* or *ture.*

2. How did I feel about my fracture? _____

_____

3. Circle the thing below that didn't happen to me in the hospital.

      I got a shot.   My arm was set.

      I was tripped.   My temperature went down.

4. Another word for recovery is im __ __ __ __ __ ment.

5. Write the word that is a synonym for *exit.* _____

_____

Lesson 6

Some endings sound alike, e.g., *-able* and *-ible*.
In this case, they both say /u-bl/ as in *wash<u>able</u>* and *terr<u>ible</u>*.

Circle the endings and write the syllables in the squares.
Note: Use the last square for the two-syllable endings, *-able* and *-ible*.

1. presentable	_ _ _	_ _ _ _	_ _ _ _	
2. miserable	_ _ _	_ _	_ _ _ _	
3. valuable	_ _ _	_	_ _ _ _	
4. impossible	_ _	_ _ _	_ _ _ _ _	
5. dependable	_ _	_ _ _ _	_ _ _ _	
6. reversible	_ _	_ _ _ _	_ _ _ _	
7. favorable	_ _	_ _ _	_ _ _ _	

Now count the syllables in each word and write the number in the margin.
Don't forget! *-able* and *-ible* are two-syllable suffixes.

Unscramble the syllables to make a word that fits the meaning.

	able to be depended on	=	pend de able	__dependable__

1. worth a lot = val / able / u _____

2. dependable = able / re / li _____

3. fantastic = in / ible / cred _____

4. not able to be seen = in / ible / vis _____

5. able to be turned inside out = vers / ible / re _____

6. astonishing = able / re / mark _____

7. able to be divided = div / is / ible _____

Circle the letters that are the same and complete the sentence with the words.

(sense) (sensible)	Rufus is a _____ **sensible** _____ dog. He seems to have a lot of common _____ **sense** _____.
1. valueless valuable	The thief did not steal my _____ ring because he thought it was _____.
2. favored unfavorable	Dad _____ going to the beach today, but the weather was _____ for swimming.
3. combust combustible	Gas and kerosene will _____, or burn, easily. They are _____ liquids.
4. depend dependable	Janet is very _____. You can always _____ on her when you need her help.
5. presented presentable	My report looked neat and _____. I _____ it orally to the class yesterday.
6. divide divisible	You can _____ twelve by six evenly. However, six is not evenly _____ by twenty.
7. wash washable	Can you _____ that shirt? I do not think that silk is _____.

44

Find the word that means the opposite of the given word(s) and write it in the boxes.

Remember: Antonyms are opposites.

miserable   uncomfortable   sensible
possible   valuable   washable
excitable   usable   divisible

1. Calm and quiet:

2. Foolish:

3. Worthless:

4. Happy:

5. Impossible:

6. Cozy:

7. Useless:

Circle the correct word below.

Look at the endings -*able* and -*ible* and think about
the words we have used with these endings.

The word *break**able*** means "_____ to be broken."

You know that -*able* and -*ible* mean "_____
to do something."

1. Is a monster movie

   possible   or   horrible?

2. If you are mowing the grass on a nice day and it starts to rain, would you
   say the weather is

   invisible   or   changeable?

3. If you have been paid to baby-sit, are you

   responsible   or   remarkable?

4. Is your new puppy

   adorable   or   available?

5. Is Mom's old tennis racket

   washable   or   usable?

6. Is a nervous person

   returnable   or   excitable?

7. If your plastic cup splits down the side when you hold it too tightly, is it

   breakable   or   valuable?

Put an X after the headline that matches each picture.

1. This Fire Was Avoidable ☐

   Adorable Baby Panda Born at Zoo ☐

2. Excitable Fans Stampede Grandstand ☐

   Incredible Picture of President Painted ☐

3. Impossible Record Broken by Supersonic Jet ☐

   Record Awards Given to Winners ☐

4. Heavy Thunderstorms Possible Tonight ☐

   Teachable Rabbit Trained to Play Music ☐

5. Solar Power Available to Homeowners ☐

   Suitable Home Found for Baby Wildcat ☐

6. Remarkable Inventor Wins Prize ☐

   Vote Close in Unpredictable Upset ☐

7. New Condo Housing Now Available ☐

   Tigers' Chance to Win Now Favorable ☐

Yes or no?

	Yes	No
1. Can a raincoat be reversible?	☐	☐
2. Are most glasses nonbreakable?	☐	☐
3. Is fried liver horrible?	☐	☐
4. Can a dry forest be combustible?	☐	☐
5. Are your grades in school improvable?	☐	☐
6. Are your books washable?	☐	☐
7. Is a fresh quart of milk returnable?	☐	☐

48

Is It Returnable?

Margie worked at a department store. Her job was processing returns. People came to her all day with things they had bought there but found unusable.

Margie was a sensible young woman with a good sense of humor. She told stories of the most remarkable returns for entertainment at parties.

One story concerned an excitable mother, her adorable toddler, and some pajamas the toddler had received. It turned out that the pajamas were flammable. "Combustible!" said the mother. "My child could have burst into flames!"

Margie agreed that the pajamas were horrible and processed the return.

A man brought back glasses that were supposed to be unbreakable. He threw one on the floor, and it broke into a dozen pieces. "Breakable indeed," said Margie and gave him his money back.

Margie's favorite story was about a woman who tried to return a sweater that she had knitted herself. "I thought it was washable," said the woman, showing Margie a shrunken sweater. Margie said, "It is NOT washable, but it is also NOT returnable, since you didn't buy it here."

1. Circle all the words that end in *able* or *ible*.

2. What was Margie's job?_____

3. How did Margie entertain her friends at parties?_____

_____

4. Which of her stories do you like most? Why did you pick that one?

_____

5. Another word that means the same thing as *flammable* is
   com __ __ __ __ ible.

Lesson 7

Other endings that do not sound the way they are spelled are *-tion* and *-sion*. These endings say /shun/ as in *na<u>tion</u>* and *mis<u>sion</u>*.

Circle the endings and write the syllables in the squares.

#					
1.	subtraction	_ _ _	_ _ _ _	_ _ _ _	
2.	invention	_ _	_ _ _	_ _ _ _	
3.	confusion	_ _ _	_ _	_ _ _ _	
4.	suggestion	_ _ _	_ _ _	_ _ _ _	
5.	starvation	_ _ _ _	_ _	_ _ _ _	
6.	expression	_ _	_ _ _ _	_ _ _ _	
7.	explosion	_ _	_ _ _	_ _ _ _	

Now say the words aloud in syllables and write the number of syllables you hear in the margin.

Unscramble the syllables to make a word that fits the meaning.

the thing chosen = tion / se / lec → selection

Remember: *-tion* and *-sion* say /shun/.

1. a disease caused by germs = tion / fec / in → _____

2. a letter inviting you to a party = vi / ta / in / tion → _____

3. consent to do something = per / sion / mis → _____

4. wearing earth away by water or wind = e / ro / sion → _____

5. a written story = po / com / si / tion → _____

6. careful listening and watching = ten / tion / at → _____

7. preventing waste or destruction of nature = ser / con / va / tion → _____

Circle the letters that are the same and complete the sentence with the words.

(collect collection)	My uncle has a __collection__ of duck decoys, but I prefer to __collect__ baseball cards myself.	
1.	add addition	I like to _____ . Perhaps that's why I'm so good at _____ .
2.	instructor instructions	After she finished giving the _____ for the test, the _____ sat down.
3.	elect election	Do you want to _____ Adams in the next _____ ?
4.	express expression	She used that awful _____ to _____ her anger at my leaving so early.
5.	televise television	We watched them _____ the children's _____ show.
6.	starve starvation	When people don't have food, they _____. This is called _____ .
7.	motion motionless	The students are _____ when they are in line. At recess the students are in _____ .

Find the word that is described and write it in the boxes.

separation   relaxation   exploration
permission   erosion   television
correction   starvation   celebration

1. A party in honor of someone or something:

2. Not having enough food to eat:

3. The wearing or washing away of earth:

4. Rest or taking it easy or not working:

5. Allowing:

6. The act of searching and discovering:

7. Parting or not being together:

Circle the correct word below.

> Look at the endings *-tion* and *-sion*.
>
> You pronouce both /_____/, as in *na<u>tion</u>* and *mis<u>sion</u>*.

1. When you are sick, does the doctor give you

   mention   or   medication?

2. When you have done your very best, do you feel

   satisfaction   or   subtraction?

3. When you give money to the hospital, do you make

   a direction   or   a donation?

4. When your boss gives you a better job with more pay, is it

   a promotion   or   a permission?

5. When you think you've solved a problem, do you have

   a solution   or   a selection?

6. When you had your tonsils out, was it

   an operation   or   a vacation?

7. If you take the train or bus to work, is it your

   composition   or   transportation?

Put an X after the headline that matches each picture.

| 1. | Exploration of Mountain Hazardous | ☐ | |
| | Election Means Mayor Will Retire | ☐ | |

| 2. | Donation Made for Hospital Wing | ☐ | |
| | Location of Gold Found 80 Years Later | ☐ | |

| 3. | Station Needs Funds to Operate | ☐ | |
| | Caution Needed on Dangerous Climb | ☐ | |

| 4. | Attention! Last Day of Sale! | ☐ | |
| | Addition Made to Starting Lineup | ☐ | |

| 5. | Mom Wins Promotion at Police Station | ☐ | |
| | Scientists Cheer Growing Eagle Population | ☐ | |

| 6. | Dog Finds Family after Separation | ☐ | |
| | Fly Ball Wins Game | ☐ | |

| 7. | Operation Successful on Hippo | ☐ | |
| | New Flag for Town Hall—A Big Occasion! | ☐ | |

Yes or no?

	Yes	No
1. Will you be sad if there is no vacation?	☐	☐
2. Is a birthday a celebration?	☐	☐
3. When you don't understand your work, is what you feel confusion?	☐	☐
4. Does a rich person live in a mansion?	☐	☐
5. Does Mother give you permission to watch television?	☐	☐
6. Have you ever won an election?	☐	☐
7. Can an otter give you swimming instructions?	☐	☐

My Vacation Blog

It's the end of the school year and time for a celebration! Sure, I'm all for getting a good education. Mr. Kline's instruction was excellent. But now it's time for vacation, and I can turn my attention to the things I enjoy most.

And most of all I love motion. For me, exploring a new location leads to happiness! I go to the train station with my family or some friends. We read the posted list of suggestions for city outings and directions for how to get to them. We choose, and the fun begins.

Secondly, I love relaxation. It's incredible to have enough time for reading my comics collection, watching my favorite television shows, and, of course, writing my blog!

Thirdly, I have a mission to be as helpful as possible in my community. I volunteer at the hospital and weed the flowerbeds in the public park. I feel good helping out.

Fourthly, there's the Fourth. No, I'm not crazy. I mean the Fourth of July. The firework explosions are almost as exciting as summer vacation itself!

1. Circle all the words that end in *tion* or *sion*.

2. Underline the words that describe what the blogger does when she travels.

3. Another word that means almost the same as *neighborhood* is com __ __ __ ity.

4. What would you write a blog about? _____

   _____

5. Do you think the blogger would like summer vacation to last all year long? Why do you think that? _____

   _____

Lesson 8 • Review

Circle the correct word.

valuable?

or

(washable?)

---

entertainment?

or

measurement?

breakable?

or

returnable?

---

filthiness?

or

famous?

furniture?

or

fracture?

---

separation?

or

disagreement?

election?

or

explosion?

---

selection?

or

subtraction?

capture?

or

manufacture?

Draw a circle around the letters that are different and fill in the blanks.

1.	slip slip(periness)	The _slipperiness_ of the floor made the waiter _slip_ .
2.	protection protector	My family does not need _____ because my dog is a good _____ .
3.	collector collection	The garbage _____ makes his _____ every Thursday morning.
4.	nature naturalist	I want to be a _____ someday because of my love of _____ .
5.	instructions instructor	I received _____ on how to drive a car from the driving school _____ .
6.	visible invisible	If something is not _____ , or cannot be seen, it is _____ .
7.	invention infections	Her new medical _____ will help fight viral _____ .

Choose and add one of the suffixes to each underlined word.

-tion   -ture   -ment   -able

When you subtract 3 from 4,

the process is called ___subtraction___ .

$$\begin{array}{r} 4 \\ -3 \\ \hline 1 \end{array}$$

Note: When you add -tion or -ture to a word that ends in t, drop one t.

1. If something <u>suit</u>s you well it is _____ .

2. They want to <u>adopt</u> a child. I hope the _____ works out.

3. This cake is <u>moist</u>. It has plenty of _____ in it.

4. Some foods are hard to <u>digest</u>. Eating slowly helps your _____ .

5. Your health seems to <u>improve</u> every day. Your _____ means that you can soon go back to school.

6. It was easy to <u>train</u> my rabbit. He is a very _____ bunny.

7. I love to be <u>entertain</u>ed. A three-ring circus is my favorite kind of

_____ .

Circle the correct meaning or definition of each underlined word.

She stared in <u>amazement</u> at the horse nibbling grass in her garden.

<u>Amazement</u> means: 1. enjoyment
　　　　　　　　　　　　 2. great surprise

1. In the darkness I saw an <u>illusion</u> that seemed to be a lion.
   <u>Illusion</u> means:　　　　1. an exact copy
   　　　　　　　　　　　　2. something unreal or imagined
   　　　　　　　　　　　　3. a picture

2. I plan to be a concert violinist in the <u>future</u>.
   <u>Future</u> means:　　　　 1. a day before yesterday
   　　　　　　　　　　　　2. last Saturday
   　　　　　　　　　　　　3. a time that is to come

3. He does everything the exact way I do it; he is an <u>imitator</u>.
   <u>Imitator</u> means:　　　　1. someone who starts a new job
   　　　　　　　　　　　　2. a mimic or one who copies another
   　　　　　　　　　　　　3. the starter of a prank

4. "Are these mushrooms <u>edible</u>?" she asked, examining them closely.
   <u>Edible</u> means:　　　　　1. salty
   　　　　　　　　　　　　2. safe to eat
   　　　　　　　　　　　　3. too hot

5. "You are very <u>suitable</u> for this job," said the smiling manager.
   <u>Suitable</u> means:　　　　1. proper; well-suited
   　　　　　　　　　　　　2. ready; on time
   　　　　　　　　　　　　3. poorly qualified

6. <u>Pollution</u> of rivers and streams is a serious problem in America.
   <u>Pollution</u> means:　　　　1. too many swimmers
   　　　　　　　　　　　　2. too many fish
   　　　　　　　　　　　　3. having become dirty and poisonous

7. My mother's new company <u>manufactures</u> computers.
   <u>Manufactures</u> means:　　1. sells
   　　　　　　　　　　　　2. investigates
   　　　　　　　　　　　　3. makes

Which word would you use to describe or name a person who:

adorable	illusion	occasion
future	equipment	captivity
connection	decision	amazement

1. — someone or something that's very cute? _____

2. — the joining of two parts? _____

3. — tomorrow and the years following? _____

4. — being held in a cage? _____

5. — the tools and supplies needed for a job? _____

6. — a special event or opportunity? _____

7. — complete surprise? _____

Find and circle the words you know and then fit them into the spaces below.

The words go across or down the page and can overlap.

```
M I N F O R M A T I O N S T
H M A T I O C L M S P O R V
U P T O W N A D O R A B L E
M O I S T U R E X P U L S X
O S O C H E E R T I C A G P
R E I L P U L Y C G K O S L
W B A M A Z E M E N T F J O
M E N T N R S V Z P H L D S
Q T I M P O S S I B L E X I
B G K S O W A Q Y I U M E O
W C A Q G M U K I O Y S E N
```

CARELESS (not careful)

H _ _ _ R (jokes)

E _ _ _ _ _ _ _ N (fireworks' result)

A _ _ _ _ _ _ E (cute and lovable)

M _ _ _ _ _ _ E (dampness)

A _ _ _ _ _ _ _ T (surprise)

I _ _ _ _ _ _ _ _ E (not possible)

I _ _ _ _ _ _ _ _ _ N (facts)

What a Way to Fly!

If you have an adventurous personality, you should try a balloon trip. Filling the balloon with hot air takes about twenty minutes. Propane torches are lighted, and the heat from them is forced into the balloon by a fan. Slowly the gigantic nylon pocket begins to inflate and to rise higher and higher. The basket at the base of the balloon, with enough room for just two or three people, is tied to the ground for security while the balloon is being inflated.

At last the balloon is ready to launch. The balloonist casts off the guide wires, and the balloon slowly rises. Blasts of hot air from the propane torches control the height the balloon will go: the more heat, the higher the flight. The wind controls the speed and direction of the flight.

It takes skill and ability on the part of the balloonist to keep from crashing into trees and telephone wires. Alertness is a necessity!

When a tree looms ahead, a blast of hot air sends the balloon upward, and a collision is avoided. Can you imagine skimming the tops of trees and peering down chimneys? This is what is known as "a bird's eye view." Happily, the majority of flights are without calamity.

A bit later the balloonist spots a green field ahead. By withholding hot air, the balloon gradually descends, setting the basket down in the green, grassy pasture. Curious neighbors from the community come from all directions to watch in amazement and to help pack the balloon back into its bag.

What a festive party they have now. The truck that has been trailing the balloon brings treats for all to share. Everyone cheers the magnificent balloon. What a glorious adventure! I wonder if ballooning tourists ever really come down to earth again.

Question Sheet

1. Circle the words that best describe a balloon trip.

   adventure   unbelievable   invisible

   enjoyable   disappointment   occasion

2. How do you fill a balloon with air?

   _____

3. Supply the correct word from the story.

   a. Safety or being secure is called _____.

   b. Watchfulness or quickness to avoid danger is called

      _____.

   c. A crash, or two things colliding, is called a _____.

   d. An event that causes great harm is a _____.

   e. Members of a town or a section of a town make up a

      _____.

4. Echo the questions. Write your answers in complete sentences.
   How does a balloonist keep from crashing into trees?

   _____

   _____

   What controls the direction and speed of a balloon?

   _____

   _____

5. Circle a smaller word in each word.

   personality   balloonist   trailing   majority
   tourists   amazement   alertness   noiselessly

6. Circle the letter of the main idea of the story.

   a. It takes skill to be a balloonist.

   b. Everyone helps pack the balloon away.

   c. It takes twenty minutes to fill a balloon with hot air.

   d. Ballooning is an exciting activity.

Lesson 9

The endings -*ance* and -*ence* have
the sound you hear in *bal<u>ance</u>*.

Circle the endings and write the syllables in the squares.

1. excellence	_ _	_ _ _	_ _ _ _ _	
2. difference	_ _ _	_ _ _	_ _ _ _	
3. ambulance	_ _	_ _	_ _ _ _ _ _	
4. influence	_ _	_ _ _	_ _ _ _	
5. defiance	_ _	_ _	_ _ _ _	
6. insurance	_ _	_ _ _	_ _ _ _	
7. audience	_ _	_ _	_ _ _ _	

Now say the words aloud in syllables and write the number of syllables you hear
in the margin.

66

Unscramble the syllables to make a word that fits the meaning.

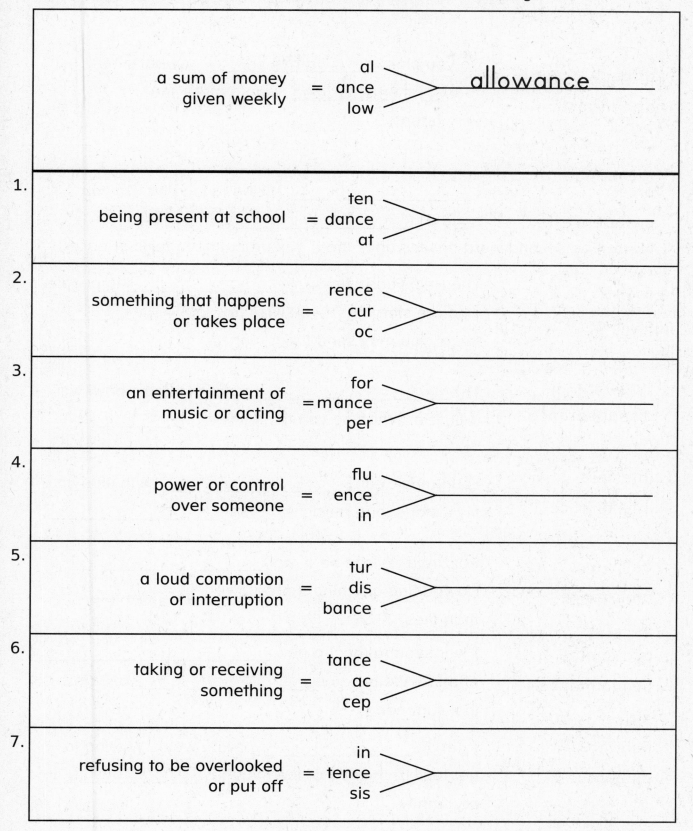

	a sum of money given weekly	= al ance low	allowance
1.	being present at school	= ten dance at	
2.	something that happens or takes place	= rence cur oc	
3.	an entertainment of music or acting	= for mance per	
4.	power or control over someone	= flu ence in	
5.	a loud commotion or interruption	= tur dis bance	
6.	taking or receiving something	= tance ac cep	
7.	refusing to be overlooked or put off	= in tence sis	

Circle the letters that are the same and complete the sentence with the words.

(attend)
(attend)ance

Do you plan to _____ **attend** _____ my party?
Your _____ **attendance** _____ would make me
very happy.

---

1. prefer

   preference

   I _____ biking to jogging. Do you
   have a _____ ?
   Note: The second word divides after the f; it is pronounced /pref-er-ence/.

---

2. assist

   assistance

   The Help Fund offers _____ to people
   who are starving. If you wish to _____
   them, you may send them money.

---

3. reappear

   disappearance

   The _____ of the dog's bowl was
   a puzzle. When do you think it will _____ ?

---

4. interfere

   interference

   Loud music can _____ with studying.
   My sister's loud music is a great _____ .

---

5. annoying

   annoyance

   Buzzing flies can be a real _____.
   Do you find anything more _____
   than flies?

---

6. acquainted

   acquaintance

   I want you to meet a new _____
   of mine. We became _____ at camp
   last summer.

---

7. allowable

   allowance

   I get an _____ every week. Waiting to
   get it all at the end of the month is _____ in
   my family.

68

Find the word that means the same as the given word(s) and write it in the boxes.

Remember: Synonyms are words that mean the same.

abundance	commence	intelligence
silence	dependence	annoyance
disappearance	elegance	performance

1. Stillness:

2. Plenty:

3. Brain power:

4. Gracefulness:

5. Vanishing:

6. To begin:

7. An irritation or a bother:

Circle the correct word below.

Remember: *-ance* and *-ence* have
the sound you hear in b__ __ __ __ __ __.

1. When something is missing, do you worry about its

      distance   or   disappearance?

2. When someone makes too much noise, is it

      a disturbance   or   a residence?

3. When you obey your parents and do what they ask, is it

      defiance   or   obedience?

4. If you are a soloist in a concert where everyone claps and cheers, are they

      your audience   or   your entrance?

5. If you found the stolen chest with fingerprints on it, do you have

      the evidence   or   the excellence?

6. When your brother keeps teasing you, is he

      an attendance   or   an annoyance?

7. If you can climb to the top of a mountain alone, do you

      have endurance   or   need assistance?

Put an X after the headline that matches each picture.

1.
Entrance to Cave Blocked by Rock ☐

Attendance at Voting Site High ☐

2.
Judge Demands Silence ☐

Judy's Performance Was Excellent ☐

3.
Football Team Runs Interference ☐

No Finance for Gold Medal Swim Team ☐

4.
Acceptance of Check by Mayor ☐

Pets Learn Obedience from Master ☐

5.
Movie Star Gives Local Boy Allowance ☐

Tomato Throwers Are an Annoyance ☐

6.
Dee Dasher: Winner of Long Distance Race ☐

Spectators Cause Disturbance at Car Race ☐

7.
Super Independence Day Celebration ☐

Abundance of Swimmers at Beach ☐

Yes or no?

		Yes	No
1.	Is it possible to walk out an entrance?	☐	☐
2.	Is there a difference between twelve and a dozen?	☐	☐
3.	Does your teacher like silence in the classroom?	☐	☐
4.	Have you had any experience in skydiving?	☐	☐
5.	Can a dry substance be gooey?	☐	☐
6.	Is it a coincidence that we were born the same day?	☐	☐
7.	Is there an abundance of ice cream in your freezer?	☐	☐

What a Difference a Dog Makes!

Winston was an adorable, playful, black Labrador pup when we got him. He loved to jump on laps and couches, nibble at ears and rugs, give kisses, and nudge elbows. He always wanted attention and an audience. We knew he needed a little guidance, but we adored him anyway.

What a difference a year makes! Winston grew much bigger, but he still had not learned obedience. When he jumped up, he knocked you flat on the floor. His kisses were juicy laps across your face, and his nudges to your elbow spilled coffee all over the floor. Winston constantly chewed holes in rugs and marked couches with muddy footprints. Our tolerance began to turn to annoyance!

One day when Winston was left home alone, he got angry. "I'll make a disturbance so that they will come back," thought Winston. When we got home there were only the shreds of evidence! Winston had eaten my homework as well as my mother's checkbook!

1. Circle all the words that end in *ance* or *ence.*

2. Underline the words that tell what Winston liked to do.

3. When one does as he or she is told and obeys commands, it is called

   o __ __ __ __ __ __ __ __ .

4. Would you say Winston needed guidance or allowance? (Circle one.)

5. If you had been me, would you have: (Circle one.)

   a. Sent Winston to school to explain about your homework?

   b. Sent Winston to school to learn his A, B, Cs?

   c. Asked Winston to lie down and grow old?

   d. Other_____

Lesson 10

The endings *-tive* and *-sive* are not pronounced the way the way they are spelled. In both cases the *e* has no effect. *-tive* says /tiv/ and *-sive* says /siv/.

Circle the endings and write the syllables in the squares.

1. attentive	_ _	_ _ _	_ _ _ _	
2. expensive	_ _	_ _ _	_ _ _ _	
3. productive	_ _ _	_ _ _	_ _ _ _	
4. detective	_ _	_ _ _	_ _ _ _	
5. defensive	_ _	_ _ _	_ _ _ _	
6. talkative	_ _ _ _	_	_ _ _ _	
7. captive		_ _ _	_ _ _ _	

Now say the words aloud in syllables and write the number of syllables you hear in the margin.

74

Unscramble the syllables to make a word that fits the meaning.

a person who solves mysteries or crimes	= tec tive de	**detective**

Remember: The endings say /tiv/ and /siv/.

1. clever, skillful, and imaginative = tive / ven / in _____

2. having a flaw or not being quite perfect = de / fec / tive _____

3. selective; fashionable = sive / ex / clu _____

4. causing a commotion or interruption = dis / tive / rup _____

5. having an effect or making an impression = im / pres / sive _____

6. easily hurt or upset = si / sen / tive _____

Remember: *i* is short before endings, even if it ends in a syllable.

7. helping to improve something = tive / con / struc _____

Circle the letters that are the same and complete the sentence with the words.

(disrupting disruptive)	The wild, __disruptive__ puppy did a good job of __disrupting__ the picnic with his barking and jumping about.	
1.	expense expensive	She went to great _____ to buy you such an _____ gift.
2.	collection recollect	If I _____ her room, it has a lovely doll _____ .
3.	captive captivity	The enemy was taken _____ and held in _____ for a long time.
4.	actor inactive	The old movie _____ lives a quiet, _____ life now.
5.	expression expressive	The happy _____ on her face was _____ of the joy she felt.
6.	impressive impression	He made a great _____ on the young girl, who thought he was a very _____ actor.
7.	produce productive	How much wheat does the United States _____ each year? United States wheat farmers are very _____ .

Find the word that is described and write it in the boxes.

massive   decorative   secretive
detective   expensive   native
impressive   creative   active

1. One of the original people of a country:

2. Very large and heavy:

3. A person who solves crimes:

4. Pretty, like an ornament:

5. Costing a great deal of money:

6. Wanting to hide or conceal something:

7. Able to make new and original things:

77

Circle the correct word below.

Remember: *-tive* and *-sive* say /tiv/ and /siv/.

active   or   (expensive)?

1. When something is too big or heavy to move, do we say it is

   massive   or   native?

2. When you do not want to do something, is your answer

   negative   or   positive?

3. If you are interested in class and pay close attention, are you

   attentive   or   expensive?

4. When you write a marvelous story with clay figures to illustrate it, are you

   festive   or   creative?

5. When a table is covered with a gold and silver cloth, do we say it is

   collective   or   decorative?

6. When you just sit quietly and read all day, do we say you are

   active   or   inactive?

7. If you tell me lots and lots about your friends and family, do we call you

   secretive   or   talkative?

Put an X after the headline that matches each picture.

1.
Enormous Lion Taken Captive ☐

Lion Cub Captures Hearts of Zoogoers ☐

2.
Creative Child Wins Art Show Prize ☐

Creator of Safety Pin Never Known ☐

3.
Expensive Painting Auctioned ☐

Extensive Trip Undertaken to South Pole ☐

4.
Primitive Inventions Discovered ☐

Sensitive Reader Saves Bird ☐

5.
Government Secretive About Plans ☐

Talkative Person Gives Secret to Spy ☐

6.
Bicyclist Disruptive at Concert ☐

Detective Arrests Conductor of Train ☐

7.
Inventive Girl Aids Walkers ☐

Naturalist Helps Save Whales ☐

79

Yes or no?

		Yes	No
1.	Is it expensive to camp in the mountains?	☐	☐
2.	Could you keep a firefly captive?	☐	☐
3.	If you're attentive, will you hear the story?	☐	☐
4.	Is a mushroom massive?	☐	☐
5.	Are you a native of your town?	☐	☐
6.	Can a necklace be decorative?	☐	☐
7.	Is your grandfather a relative?	☐	☐

Undersea Detectives

Excited by our hunt for unusual undersea life, we jumped into our jeep. With snorkel masks and flippers, we headed for a secluded bay with extensive reefs. Once we were in the blue-green water, attractive schools of purple angelfish, trumpetfish, blue tang, and butterfly fish surrounded us. Giant white sea urchins waved to us from the coral formations. We were a captive audience! My sister poked me and pointed. A massive grouper fish was making faces at us. We searched on through the decorative coral. It was impressive to be among hundreds of midnight blue parrotfish. We were so attentive that we never realized how far out we had swum.

Suddenly there he was—a fierce, ugly jawed barracuda with teeth like saws! I grabbed my sister's toe and motioned to her. Then slowly and silently, so as not to be disruptive, I started back to shore. It seemed miles away.

1. Circle all the words that end in *tive* or *sive*.

2. Underline the words that tell what kind of bay it was.

3. If you make a lot of noise or commotion, you are said to be
d __ __ __ __ __ tive.

4. Would you say that the swim back to shore was active or inactive?
(Circle one.)

5. If you had been me, what would you have done? (Circle one.)

   a. Left your sister and swum back to shore full speed ahead?

   b. Tapped the barracuda on the back and told him he needed a good dentist?

   c. Pinched yourself to try and awaken from the bad dream?

   d. Other_____

   _____

Lesson 11

-ify and -ize are endings. -ify is a two-syllable ending pronounced /ĭ-fī/, as in noti**fy**.

Circle the endings and write the syllables in the squares.
Use the last square for the two-syllable ending, -ify.

1. ratify   _ _ _   _ _ _

2. solidify   _ _   _ _ _   _ _ _

3. modernize   _ _ _   _ _ _   _ _ _

4. memorize   _ _ _   _   _ _ _ _

5. qualify   _ _ _ _   _ _ _

6. motorize   _ _   _ _ _   _ _ _

7. finalize   _ _   _ _ _   _ _ _

Now say the words aloud in syllables and write the number of syllables you hear in the margin.

Unscramble the syllables to make a word that fits the meaning.

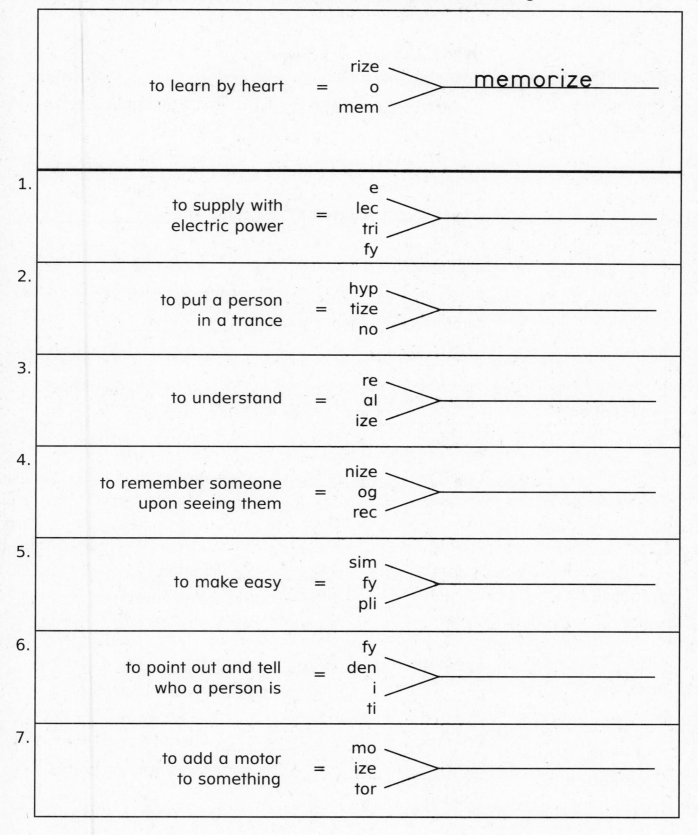

	to learn by heart	=	rize o mem ⟩ memorize
1.	to supply with electric power	=	e lec tri fy ⟩ _____
2.	to put a person in a trance	=	hyp tize no ⟩ _____
3.	to understand	=	re al ize ⟩ _____
4.	to remember someone upon seeing them	=	nize og rec ⟩ _____
5.	to make easy	=	sim fy pli ⟩ _____
6.	to point out and tell who a person is	=	fy den i ti ⟩ _____
7.	to add a motor to something	=	mo ize tor ⟩ _____

Circle the letters that are the same and complete the sentence with the words.

(memory) (memorize)	If you have a good _____ memory _____ , you can _____ memorize _____ lots of facts and dates.	
1.	visual visualize	If you can see a _____ image of something in your mind, you can _____ it.
2.	simple simplify	When you _____ the directions to something, you make them _____ .
3.	realize realization	We came to the _____ that you did not _____ we were lost.
4.	motorist motorized	Could a _____ drive a _____ bike?
5.	critic criticize	A drama _____ will often _____ the actors in the show.
6.	note notify	I sent her a _____ to _____ her of the fire drill on Friday.
7.	apology apologize	When you _____ , you give someone an _____ for something you are sorry you did.

84

Find the word that is described and write it in the boxes.

Remember: The suffix *-ify* says /___-____/, as in *notify*.

electrify	memorize	magnify
identify	qualify	realize
apologize	simplify	hypnotize

These words are all things you can do.

1. To add electricity to something:

2. To say you are sorry:

3. To make bigger:

4. To learn by heart:

5. To make easier:

6. To point out or name:

7. To show enough skill to be on a team:

Circle the correct word below.

Remember the endings *-ize* and *-ify*
as you read the words below.

capitalize   or   (magnify)?

1. When you are sorry for something, do you

   apologize   or   identify?

2. When you want to put someone in a trance, do you

   criticize them   or   hypnotize them?

3. When you want to learn something and remember it, do you

   magnify it   or   memorize it?

4. When you see someone you know, do you

   motorize him   or   recognize him?

5. When you want to make something new and up-to-date, do you

   modernize it   or   notify it?

6. When you want to make something more attractive, do you

   beautify it   or   jellify it?

7. When you melt something to make it liquid, do you

   liquefy it   or   solidify it?

   Note: *Liquefy* uses *-efy* instead of *-ify*.

Put an X after the headline that matches each picture.

1. Doctor Sterilizes Instruments ☐

   Doctor Adopts Baby Skunk ☐

2. Girl Recognizes Picture of Twin Sister ☐

   Revolution Breaks Out ☐

3. President Gets Introduction to Queen ☐

   Turtle Gets Instructions for Road Race ☐

4. Experts Realize Bones Are Dinosaur's ☐

   Election Returns Come in Late ☐

5. Reading Teachers Simplify Classwork ☐

   Class Accepts Invitation to Washington ☐

6. Valuable Art Collection Missing! ☐

   Zoo to Modernize ☐

7. Star Gets Motorized Shopping Cart ☐

   Ringmaster Jealous of Circus Clown ☐

Yes or no?

	Yes	No
1. Can you liquefy butter?	☐	☐
2. Can you hypnotize your teacher?	☐	☐
3. Can the dentist notify me by mail if she wants me to make an appointment?	☐	☐
4. Will you apologize to your cat if you step on her tail?	☐	☐
5. Would you recognize your grandmother?	☐	☐
6. Can you visualize a double-dip peppermint ice cream cone?	☐	☐
7. Would you electrify popcorn before you popped it?	☐	☐

Long Time, No See

Paul and Frank were cousins. A long time had passed since they'd seen each other, but finally, Paul was visiting Frank.

"I apologize for not staying in touch," said Paul. "I almost didn't recognize you when you answered the door!"

"I hope you realize that we are both to blame," said Frank. "I didn't notify you until long after I moved."

"Well, I can't criticize you for that," said Paul. "You've probably been awfully busy."

"I have," Frank said. "I had to modernize and beautify this house before I invited guests. There was no electricity here. I had to electrify the place. See if you can visualize how old-fashioned it was. Imagine—no lights, no refrigerator, no television, no computer access! Worst of all, there was no way to play video games. You wouldn't have come for a visit!"

"That's true, Cousin," said Paul, with a smile. "Sad, but true."

1. Circle all the words that end in *ize* or *ify*.

2. How are Paul and Frank related? _____

3. If you picture something in your mind, you v __ __ __ __ __ ize it.

4. Name some things that were missing from Frank's house before he modernized it. _____

_____

5. Do you think Paul and Frank had played video games together before Frank moved? Why do you think that? _____

_____

_____

Lesson 12

ti- and *ci-* before an ending say /sh/. The rest of the letters have their usual sounds. For example:

  -tian and *-cian* = /shan/   *-tient* and *-cient* = /shent/
  -tious and *-cious* = /shus/

Circle the endings and write the syllables. Remember: *i* before endings is usually short even though it ends the syllable.

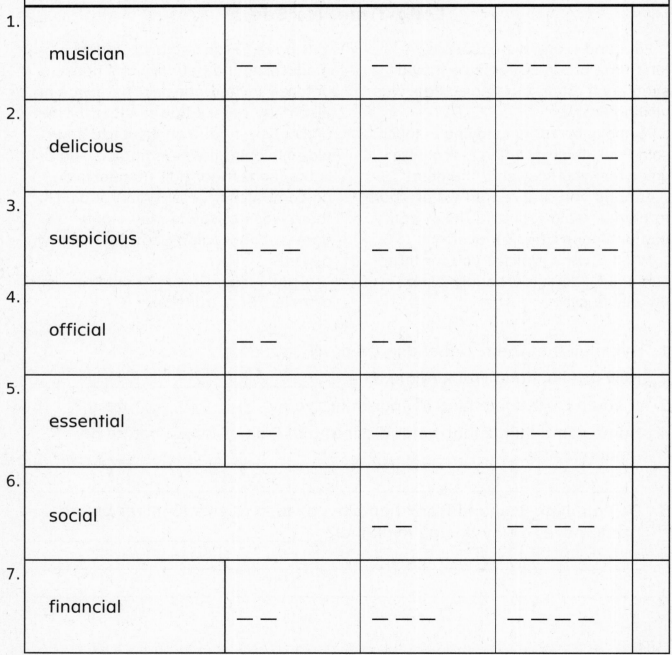

1. musician _ _   _ _   _ _ _ _ _

2. delicious _ _   _ _   _ _ _ _ _

3. suspicious _ _ _   _ _   _ _ _ _ _ _

4. official _ _   _ _   _ _ _ _

5. essential _ _   _ _ _   _ _ _ _

6. social   _ _   _ _ _ _

7. financial _ _   _ _ _   _ _ _ _

Now say the words aloud in syllables and write the number of syllables you hear in the margin.

Unscramble the syllables to make a word that fits the meaning.

someone from the
planet Mars = tian
Mar > Martian _____

Remember: *ti-* and *ci-* say /sh/.

1. very good to eat = cious
lus > _____

2. showing distrust = sus
pi
cious > _____

3. showing calm self-control
or willing to wait = tient
pa > _____

4. friendly and liking
to be with people = cial
so > _____

5. having to do with
money and finances = fi
nan
cial > _____

6. careful = tious
cau > _____

7. most important = sen
es
tial > _____

Circle the letters that are the same and complete the sentence with the words.

Remember: These endings, *-cient*, *-tient*, *-cian*, *-tian*, *-cious*, *-tious*, *-cial*, and *-tial*, all begin with the sound of /_____/.

(Mars
Martians)   __Martians__ come from the planet
             __Mars__ .

1. office
   official

   The young government _____ has a
   new _____ to work in.

2. music
   musician

   A _____ plays
   _____ .

3. finances
   financial

   My _____ advisor knows all about
   _____ .

4. caution
   cautious

   If you are _____, you proceed with
   carefulness and _____ .

5. politics
   politician

   A _____ is always active in
   _____ .

6. electric
   electrician

   An _____ can fix all the
   _____ wires in your house.

7. part
   partial

   If I give you _____ of what I owe, I will
   have made a _____ payment.

Find the word that is described and write it in the boxes.

Do you remember what *-ti* and *-ci* say before endings? /_____/

delicious   artificial   repetitious
financial   patient   social
suspicious   Martian   essential

1. Expressing distrust:

2. Important and necessary:

3. Not natural but made by humans:

4. Luscious and pleasant tasting:

5. Repeating over and over:

6. Having to do with money:

7. A person having medical treatment:

Circle the correct word below.

Remember: *ti-* and *ci-* before an ending say /sh/.
The rest of the letters have their usual sound.

(politician)   or   caution?

1. If you bake a cake, would it be

   delicious   or   ambitious?

2. When you see someone sneaking around the house, are you

   social   or   suspicious?

3. When you have a birthday party, is it

   spacious   or   special?

4. Is doing your homework

   partial   or   essential?

5. If you are an organist and a violinist, are you

   a Martian   or   a musician?

6. When you cross a busy street, are you

   cautious   or   luscious?

7. Is the umpire

   an official   or   an electrician?

Put an X after the headline that matches each picture.

1.	Influential Musician Comes to Town	☐	
	City Politician Has No Influence on Election	☐	
2.	Martians Land in New York	☐	
	Musician Plays Last Concert	☐	
3.	Lawyer Suspicious of Partner	☐	
	Lawyer Cautious with Gravy	☐	
4.	Social Studies Book Is Done!	☐	
	Social Workers Find Dogs to Help the Blind	☐	
5.	Special All-American Game Tonight	☐	
	New Hotel Is Spacious and Lovely	☐	
6.	Pianist's Delicious Recipes Published	☐	
	Patient Comes Home from Hospital	☐	
7.	Official Demands Overtime for Game	☐	
	Author Writes Repetitious Book	☐	

95

Yes or no?

		Yes	No
1.	Does a politician wish for votes?	☐	☐
2.	Is this book repetitious?	☐	☐
3.	Are you cautious when you ride your bike on the street?	☐	☐
4.	Have you ever shaken hands with a Martian?	☐	☐
5.	Is an ice cream soda luscious?	☐	☐
6.	Do you initial your papers?	☐	☐
7.	Can you cook delicious food?	☐	☐

Roodle

My family has a very special dog. He is partially Jack Russell terrier and partially toy poodle. The mixture is called Jack-a-Poo, and we call ours Roodle, because he was very rude when he was a puppy.

We had to be very patient as Roodle grew up. Initially, his barking drove us crazy. But if he was quiet, we became suspicious. What was he up to?

When friends came to visit, we urged them to be cautious. We'd say, "Roodle is a totally unsociable dog." If they still wanted to pet him, we'd say, "You have to be reckless to touch that dog." If they insisted, we'd say, "You decide if you'd like a painful nip, but we don't recommend it."

But our patience paid off. The repetitious warning "No, Roodle!" and the frequent praise phrase "Good boy, Roodle!" proved to be all the essential training Roodle needed. Today, he is a remarkably well-behaved member of our family, a real social animal!

1. Circle all the words that have *ci-* or *ti-* before the ending.

2. Underline the word that describes Roodle when he was a puppy.

3. What did Roodle's family tell visitors?_____

_____

4. How did the family train Roodle? _____

_____

5. Someone who doesn't like company is un __ __ __ __ able.

Lesson 13 • Review

Circle the correct word.

invitation

or

(musician?)

entrance?

or

elegance?

electrician?

or

expensive?

luscious?

or

cautious?

capsize?

or

capture?

secretive?

or

structure?

moisture?

or

Martian?

magnify?

or

capsize?

attendance?

or

ambulance?

Draw a circle around the letters that are different and fill in the blanks.

1. **secret(s)** / **secret(ive)**

Jay is very ___secretive___.
He only tells his best pal his
___secrets___.

2. questions / questionable

It is _____ whether her
_____ will ever be answered.

3. illustrator / illustrations

An _____ is one who draws
the _____ in a book like this.

4. presents / representative

Your _____ in Congress
_____ your ideas to the
government.

5. dependable / independence

The farmers were _____
soldiers when they fought for their
_____ from the British.

6. patient / patience

He was very _____ with
his little sister. In most ways, he has a lot of
_____ with everyone.

7. information / informative

Your _____ was very
_____.

Choose and add one of the suffixes to each underlined word.

-ance -ize -ible -ous -ist

Funny stories told with <u>humor</u> are ___humorous___.

1. Always use a <u>capital</u> letter at the beginning of a sentence. Be sure to _____ those letters.

2. These two sections are not <u>equal</u>. Can you _____ them?

3. You can <u>flex</u> your muscle because muscles are very _____.

4. Sometimes you are <u>allow</u>ed to go to the store and use your _____ to buy candy.

5. One who plays a <u>violin</u> is a _____.

6. If you are very brave and have a lot of <u>courage</u>, you are _____.

7. When you <u>perform</u> in a fantastic bike stunt, your friends cheer your _____.

Circle the correct meaning or definition of each underlined word.

Remember: *-tious* says /shus/.
-cial says /shal/.

My grandmother is a <u>patient</u> at the general hospital.
<u>Patient</u> means:
1. a nurse
2. a person being treated
3. a janitor

1. The new senator, who was very <u>ambitious</u>, hoped to become president.
<u>Ambitious</u> means:
1. eager for advancement
2. eager for things to stay the same
3. prosperous, wealthy

2. We are polluting our <u>environment</u>.
<u>Environment</u> means:
1. rivers
2. basements
3. surroundings

3. We now have <u>disposable</u> bottles, napkins, and diapers.
<u>Disposable</u> means:
1. not having to be ironed
2. easily cleaned
3. able to be thrown away after using

4. She made a <u>gesture</u> that told me she was tired.
<u>Gesture</u> means:
1. a horrible sound
2. a movement or motion of one's hands or body
3. a smile

5. The TV show on whales was very <u>informative</u>.
<u>Informative</u> means:
1. curious
2. necessary
3. full of ideas

6. Exercise is <u>beneficial</u> to your health.
<u>Beneficial</u> means:
1. helpful
2. destructive
3. not necessary

7. <u>Evaporation</u> occurs when you boil water.
<u>Evaporation</u> means:
1. liquid turning into vapor
2. liquid getting cold
3. liquid turning to a solid

Which word would you use to describe or name a person who:

reliable   florist   desirable

nonreturnable   relatives   impatient

beneficial   immovable   patient

1. — a person who sells flowers? _____

2. — all your uncles and aunts? _____

3. — something you want very much? _____

4. — something you bought and cannot take back? _____

5. — something that won't budge? _____

6. — someone dependable whom you can always trust? _____

7. — someone who is restless and can't wait? _____

Find and circle the words you know and then fit them into the spaces below.

The words go across or down the page and can overlap.

```
C A P T U R E Q U A T E A D H
X T P C L I Q U O T A T I O N
B X F O T J U P N L R H V D Z
W C S U G P A T I E N C E K O
F L O R I S T A U E Y O I Q M
C U G A M I O E K Q W N O A S
H L Z G V Y R F B U R F J N D
B X P E N V I R O N M E N T T
K U C O Z G E L G Q J R V A P
R D M U I O S N Y U H E X T C
W L B S R G N X H D V N J B P
T H D N Z T V F X B L C P R J
E P F V L B R H X N D E Y J Y
```

C A P T U R E (to catch something)

F _ _ _ _ _ T (a flower seller)

E _ _ _ _ _ _ R (an imaginary circle around the earth)

P _ _ _ _ _ _ E (state of being patient)

Q _ _ _ _ _ _ _ _ N (something that is quoted)

C _ _ _ _ _ _ _ _ _ E (a meeting to discuss something)

C _ _ _ _ _ _ _ _ S (brave)

E _ _ _ _ _ _ _ _ _ _ T (surroundings)

103

An SUV on Firm Foundation

Before we knew it was destructive to the fragile environment, I used to drive my SUV over the sand dunes on Cape Cod. One day, some relatives were visiting, and we decided to explore an area called Race Point. I was a capable driver with lots of experience, so I was unquestionably confident.

Late in the afternoon, we arrived at Race Point. Before driving out on the beach, we removed some air from the tires. Softer tires get better traction in the sand. The endless hills and valleys of sand were spectacular. We drove over and around them. It was perfection until I realized that there were no trails to follow—just sand, sand, and endless sand. Soon, I lost my sense of direction, and the ground seemed softer than usual, but the impatient relatives in the back seat urged me on despite my confusion.

At last we saw water and drove out close to it. Suddenly, without warning, two of the tires sank deep into the fine sand, leaving our SUV perched at an uncomfortable angle next to the sea. My dependable SUV was immovable! My talkative guests grew silent. The sand here was much finer than I had ever driven on, and I should never have gone so close to the water. I should have been more cautious. Unfortunately, the tide was coming in, and I had no wish to abandon my beloved vehicle to a future at sea. Besides, it was getting late, and I knew our family at home would be frantic.

So, with a nervous but courageous spirit, I removed more air from my tires and gestured for my riders to climb out. Now with a lightened load, I once again climbed behind the wheel. The engine roared, but there was no motion. Then, ever so slowly, the vehicle began to move. Inch by inch, it crept toward firmer ground. Such cheering and celebration you have never seen! Our reliable SUV was saved, and so were we.

Question Sheet

1. Circle the words that best describe the SUV.

   reliable   essential   horrible

   victorious   remarkable   numerous

2. Explain why we don't drive on the dunes today.

   _____

   _____

3. Supply the correct word from the story.

   a. Unwilling to wait any longer: _____

   b. Unable to be moved: _____

   c. Members of one's family: _____

   d. Motioned with one's hand: _____

   e. Using care: _____

4. Echo the questions. Write your answers in complete sentences.

   What do you do to the tires before going out on the beach?

   _____

   _____

   Why did we have unexpected trouble at Race Point?

   _____

   _____

5. Circle a smaller word in each word.

   unquestionably   dependable   talkative   transportation

   directions   uncomfortable   perfection   courageous

6. Circle the letter of the main idea of the story.

   a. Relatives need to be entertained.

   b. Driving dune buggies can be exciting.

   c. Think and use caution on any kind of adventure.

   d. An SUV is good transportation at the beach.

Draw a line to the word that is in some way related.

acquainted   dexterity

dexterous   hazard

fortify   investigation

defective   acquaintance

investigator   fortification

hazardous   defection

destructive   recollection

production   impatient

patience   independence

dependent   activity

inactive   indestructible

collective   reproductive

Word Meaning

Circle the endings in the first list, and draw a line to the **synonym,** or word that means the same, in the second list.

1.	essential	celebration
2.	improvement	costly
3.	luscious	necessary
4.	festivity	bother
5.	expensive	advancement
6.	annoyance	marvelous
7.	fabulous	delicious

Circle the endings in the first list, and draw a line to the **antonym,** or word that means the opposite, in the second list.

1.	cautious	trusting
2.	attractive	reckless
3.	captivity	reward
4.	active	horrible
5.	disagreement	freedom
6.	suspicious	understanding
7.	punishment	inactive

Can you summarize it? Circle the best answer.

1. Jacky loved to swing from trees, run down hills, climb on walls, jump over streams, and splash in puddles. What kind of girl was she?

   cautious   ambitious   inactive   attentive   active

2. Everywhere along the beach for miles you could see coconut palm trees. What could you say about the coconut trees?

   expensive   assistance   abundance   poisonous   hazardous

3. A few things, such as water, are necessary for people to live. What could you say about water?

   mixture   essential   desirous   emptiness   effective

4. Lester can make a facial expression and walk in a way that looks exactly like our teacher. What is Lester?

   idealist   spectator   advisor   realist   imitator

5. The plastics plant dumps all its waste in the river. What is the plastics plant guilty of?

   possession   pollution   permission   protection   production

6. The gymnast can do backbends, splits, side rollovers, and handstands. What is the gymnast?

   sensible   personable   favorable   flexible   breakable

7. This community has many parks and gardens, a lovely new library, a huge arts center, and several new fire trucks. What is true about this community?

   prosperous   obvious   enormous   thunderous   courteous

Can you supply the missing word?

reservation   conservation   observation   starvation

1. When you want to see planes land, you go to the
_____ tower.

2. When you go to a resort on vacation, you need a _____.

3. People who do not have enough food to eat may suffer from
_____ .

4. When you don't like to see our natural environment destroyed, you are
interested in _____ .

expressive   impressive   oppressive

1. If the heat and humidity are terrible, the weather is
_____ .

2. The vast and remarkable Grand Canyon is _____.

3. If you are talkative and imaginative, we say that you are
_____ .

preference   interference   difference   reference   indifference

1. A dictionary is a _____ book.

2. When two things are not alike, there is a _____.

3. If you like fudge better than caramel, you have a
_____ .

4. If you don't care which you have, you feel _____ .

5. When the game must be stopped for some reason, it is called
_____ .